My Planner

Name	
Date	

When I become incapacitated or have died, this planner will be your guide.
Turn to **Section 1**, *Instructions*, for what to do and when.

Table of Contents

Instructions

This section is the **road map to my planner.**

It is organized to help you through the next days, weeks, and months—outlining what you need to do and where you will find the information you need.

Most of the tasks will apply whether I am incapacitated or have died—though how you handle a task may vary depending upon the circumstances.

First, if I am incapacitated, there are two important tasks:

If I Am Incapacitated
Review Health Care Directives   Applicable: ☐ Yes ☐ No
☐ **Health Care Directives.** Turn to Section 11 for information about documents I have made to direct my health care.
Review Power of Attorney for Finances   Applicable: ☐ Yes ☐ No
☐ **Durable Power of Attorney for Finances.** Turn to Section 12 for information about the document that names someone to manage my finances for me.

Now follow the outline for **Days 1 and 2**—whether I am incapacitated or have died.

Next week, complete the tasks in **Week 2.**

Within the next month, get started on the tasks in **Month 1 and Beyond**.

Days 1 and 2

These are some of the important tasks you will have to handle in the first 48 hours following my incapacity or death.

Care for Children   Applicable: ☐ Yes ☐ No

☐ **Children.** Turn to Section 4 for details about the children who rely on me for care.

Care for Others   Applicable: ☐ Yes ☐ No

☐ **Others Who Depend on Me.** Turn to Section 5 for details about other people who rely on me for care.

Care for Animals   Applicable: ☐ Yes ☐ No

☐ **Pets and Livestock.** Turn to Section 6 for information about taking care of my animals, including my wishes for placing them with others.

Contact Employer Applicable: ☐ Yes ☐ No

☐ **Employment.** Notify my employer of my incapacity or death. See Section 7 for contact information and other details about my current employment and my employment history.

Contact Business Applicable: ☐ Yes ☐ No

☐ **Business Interests.** Notify any business partners or key employees of my incapacity or death. See Section 8 for contact information and details about my current and former business interests.

Make Final Arrangements

After my death, please review these five tasks before making any final arrangements.

☐ **Arrange for the Death Certificate.** Those in charge of handling my estate will need certified copies of my death certificate to wrap up business with insurance companies, banks, the Social Security Administration, and others.

As you make arrangements for the disposition of my body, you will be asked to provide information for the death certificate. The Biographical Information section of my planner (Section 3) contains the information you will need. At this time, you should request multiple certified copies of the death certificate; you may need as many as ten.

If you are unable to request copies of my death certificate while making final arrangements, you can get them later. To find out where to send your request, go to the National Center for Health Statistics website, www.cdc.gov/nchs/w2w.htm, and click the link for the state where I died.

☐ **Organ or Body Donation.** Turn to Section 13 for my wishes about donating my body, organs, or tissues—as well as information about any plans I have already made.

☐ **Burial or Cremation.** Turn to Section 14 for details about burial or cremation, including my wishes and information about any plans I have already made.

☐ **Funeral and Memorial Services.** Turn to Section 15 for details about my funeral, memorial, or related services, including my wishes and information about any plans I have already made.

☐ **Obituary.** Turn to Section 16 for details about publishing my obituary.

Contact Family and Friends

☐ Contact all friends and relatives who should know of my incapacity or death.

If you will hold a funeral or memorial service in the next few days, contact everyone who might attend. (See Section 15 for my wishes about whom to invite.) Others will learn of my passing only by reading the obituary, if published.

Except for those who need to know about my death right away, it will help to make any arrangements for services before you make phone calls—then you won't have to call everyone twice.

You can find names and contact information for family and friends in the following locations:

_____

_____

_____

_____

_____

_____

_____

_____

_____

☐ **Protect the House.** My obituary or death notice may serve to alert thieves that the house is empty. If necessary, arrange for a neighbor, a familiar service provider (see Section 10), a church member, or the reception caterer to be at the house during services.

Review Appointment Calendar

☐ Review my calendar and cancel any scheduled appointments. You can find my calendar in the following locations:

_____

_____

_____

Manage Mail and Newspaper

☐ Pick up my mail. See Section 23 for access information, if needed. File a mail forwarding order with USPS.

☐ Cancel my newspaper subscriptions, if any. See Section 22 for payment and account information.

Read My Last Letters

☐ **Letter to Loved Ones.** As time permits, please see Section 2 for my last letters to those closest to me.

Additional Notes

_____

_____

_____

_____

_____

_____

_____

_____

_____

_____

Week 2

This section outlines the essential tasks you should handle in the two weeks following my incapacity or death.

Locate Will or Other Estate Planning Documents

☐ **Will and Trust**. After my death, see Section 17 for information about my will, trusts, or other estate planning documents that I have made.

Contact Organizations and Service Providers

Please notify financial institutions, brokers, government agencies, and others with whom I do business that I have become incapacitated or have died. The following sections will help you:

☐ **Insurance.** Turn to Section 18 for information about my insurance agents and policies. The information there will help you claim benefits, cancel, or continue coverage as appropriate.

☐ **Bank and Brokerage Accounts.** Turn to Section 19 for financial institution contact information and details about my bank and brokerage accounts.

☐ **Retirement Plans and Pensions.** Turn to Section 20 for information about my retirement and pension plan accounts, including contact information for the administrators.

☐ **Government Benefits.** Turn to Section 21 for details about my Social Security and other government benefits, including contact information for each agency.

☐ **Service Providers.** Turn to Section 10 for information about service providers, including medical, personal, and household care providers.

☐ **Other:**

_____

_____

_____

☐ **Other:**

_____

_____

_____

☐ **Other:**

_____

_____

_____

☐ **Other:**

_____

_____

_____

Review Current Bills and Accounts

- ☐ **Credit Cards and Debts.** Please review my current bills to be sure they are paid on time. Cancel and close accounts as necessary. See Section 22 for more information.

- ☐ **Secured Places and Passwords.** Turn to Section 23 for help with locked or password-protected products, services, and accounts.

Additional Notes

_____

_____

_____

_____

_____

_____

_____

_____

_____

_____

_____

_____

Working Through Grief

Whether my death was sudden or long in coming, you will experience loss after I'm gone. You may grieve for weeks, months, or even years. Grieving is uniquely personal; your grief may not mirror that of other family and friends.

During the grieving process it is normal to feel strong emotions, such as deep sadness, despair, or anger. You may even go through a time of depression.

You will heal more quickly and completely if you share your grief with supportive people—family members, friends, your faith community, therapists or physicians, or grief support groups. To find a local group (and helpful information) consult your health care providers or visit these organizations online:

- Caring Info (www.caringinfo.org or 800-658-8898)
- Legacy Connect (www.connect.legacy.com)
- Mental Health America (www.mentalhealthamerica.net or 800-273-TALK(8255)).

Month 1 and Beyond

Following is a list of tasks that you should initiate in the first month or two following my incapacity or death.

Take Inventory

☐ **Real Estate.** Turn to Section 25 for details about any real estate that I own or rent.

☐ **Vehicles.** Turn to Section 26 for information about all vehicles that I own.

☐ **Other Income and Personal Property.** Turn to Section 27 for information about important sources of income or items of personal property not described elsewhere in my planner.

☐ **Other Information.** See Section 28 for any other details that I feel you need to know.

Cancel Memberships and Driver's License

☐ **Memberships and Communities.** Over time, you will want to cancel my memberships with various organizations. See Section 9 for contact information.

☐ **Driver's License.** Notify the state motor vehicles department of my death and cancel my license. See Section 3 for my driver's license information. Also, please turn in my handicap placard, if I had one.

Prepare Tax Returns

☐ **Taxes.** Section 24 will help you gather the information you need to prepare my final tax returns. Keep returns and related records for seven years.

Additional Notes

_____

_____

_____

_____

_____

_____

Where to Get Help

As you work through the steps you must take to wrap up my affairs, you will find a number of sources for help. Where applicable, the various sections of my planner list lawyers, accountants, or others who can help with each task.

For general guidance, you may want to turn to *The Executor's Guide: Settling a Loved One's Estate or Trust*, by Mary Randolph (Nolo). It provides a detailed explanation of an executor's or successor trustee's duties.

Letter to Loved Ones

To: _____

_____

_____

_____

_____

_____

If you're reading this, it is because I am incapacitated and no longer able to manage my own affairs, or because I have passed away.

Thoughts About My Death

_____

_____

_____

_____

_____

_____

_____

_____

_____

_____

_____

_____

_____

_____

_____

_____

_____

Messages for My Loved Ones

_____

_____

_____

_____

_____

_____

_____

_____

_____

_____

_____

_____

_____

My Last Words to You

_____

_____

_____

_____

_____

_____

_____

_____

_____

_____

_____

Signature

_____

Biographical Information

In this section, you will find important personal information about me and those closest to me. You may need these vital statistics for a number of tasks, such as preparing my death certificate, writing my obituary, filing tax returns, and distributing assets to my beneficiaries.

Residence Information

Name	
Address	
Telephone(s)	
Resident of City Since (year)	
Resident of State Since (year)	

Self and Parents

	Self	Mother	Father	Stepmother	Stepfather
First Name					
Middle Name					
Last Name					
Maiden Name					
Date of Birth					
Birthplace (City, State, County, Country)					
Location of Birth Certificate					
Location of Adoption Documents					
Social Security Number					
Location of Social Security Card					
Driver's License Number and State					
Military Service: Country and Branch					

	Self	Mother	Father	Stepmother	Stepfather
Military Rank					
Military Induction Date					
Military Discharge Date					
Military Citations					
Location of Military Documents					
Date of First Marriage					
First Spouse's Name					
Location of Marriage Certificate					
Date of Divorce, Annulment, Legal Separation, or Death					
Location of Documents					
Date of Second Marriage					
Second Spouse's Name					
Location of Marriage Certificate					
Date of Divorce, Annulment, Legal Separation, or Death					
Location of Documents					
Date of Third Marriage					
Third Spouse's Name					
Location of Marriage Certificate					
Date of Divorce, Annulment, Legal Separation, or Death					
Location of Documents					
Date of Death					
Location of Death Certificate					
Address					
Telephone(s)					
Email					
Other					
Other					
Other					

Spouse or Partner

	Spouse #1	Spouse #2	Spouse #3		
First Name					
Middle Name					
Last Name					
Maiden Name					
Date of Birth					
Birthplace (City, State, County, Country)					
Location of Birth Certificate					
Location of Adoption Documents					
Social Security Number					
Location of Social Security Card					
Driver's License Number and State					
Military Service: Country and Branch					
Military Rank					
Military Induction Date					
Military Discharge Date					
Military Citations					
Location of Military Documents					
Date of First Marriage					
First Spouse's Name					
Location of Marriage Certificate					
Date of Divorce, Annulment, Legal Separation, or Death					
Location of Documents					
Date of Second Marriage					
Second Spouse's Name					
Location of Marriage Certificate					
Date of Divorce, Annulment, Legal Separation, or Death					

	Spouse #1	Spouse #2	Spouse #3		
Location of Documents					
Date of Third Marriage					
Third Spouse's Name					
Location of Marriage Certificate					
Date of Divorce, Annulment, Legal Separation, or Death					
Location of Documents					
Date of Death					
Location of Death Certificate					
Address					
Telephone(s)					
Email					
Other					
Other					
Other					

Children

	Child #1	Child #2	Child #3	Child #4	Child #5
First Name					
Middle Name					
Last Name					
Maiden Name					
Date of Birth					
Birthplace (City, State, County, Country)					
Location of Birth Certificate					
Location of Adoption Documents					
Social Security Number					
Location of Social Security Card					
Driver's License Number and State					

Children, continued

	Child #1	Child #2	Child #3	Child #4	Child #5
Military Service: Country and Branch					
Military Rank					
Military Induction Date					
Military Discharge Date					
Military Citations					
Location of Military Documents					
Date of First Marriage					
First Spouse's Name					
Location of Marriage Certificate					
Date of Divorce, Annulment, Legal Separation, or Death					
Location of Documents					
Date of Second Marriage					
Second Spouse's Name					
Location of Marriage Certificate					
Date of Divorce, Annulment, Legal Separation, or Death					
Location of Documents					
Date of Third Marriage					
Third Spouse's Name					
Location of Marriage Certificate					
Date of Divorce, Annulment, Legal Separation, or Death					
Location of Documents					
Date of Death					
Location of Death Certificate					
Address					
Telephone(s)					
Email					

Children, continued

Other					
Other					
Other					

Siblings

	Sibling #1	Sibling #2	Sibling #3	Sibling #4	Sibling #5
First Name					
Middle Name					
Last Name					
Maiden Name					
Date of Birth					
Birthplace (City, State, County, Country)					
Location of Birth Certificate					
Location of Adoption Documents					
Social Security Number					
Location of Social Security Card					
Driver's License Number and State					
Military Service: Country and Branch					
Military Rank					
Military Induction Date					
Military Discharge Date					
Military Citations					
Location of Military Documents					
Date of First Marriage					
First Spouse's Name					
Location of Marriage Certificate					
Date of Divorce, Annulment, Legal Separation, or Death					

Siblings, continued

	Sibling #1	Sibling #2	Sibling #3	Sibling #4	Sibling #5
Location of Documents					
Date of Second Marriage					
Second Spouse's Name					
Location of Marriage Certificate					
Date of Divorce, Annulment, Legal Separation, or Death					
Location of Documents					
Date of Third Marriage					
Location of Marriage Certificate					
Third Spouse's Name					
Date of Divorce, Annulment, Legal Separation, or Death					
Location of Documents					
Date of Death					
Location of Death Certificate					
Address					
Telephone(s)					
Email					
Other					
Other					
Other					

Others

First Name					
Middle Name					
Last Name					
Maiden Name					

Others, continued

Date of Birth					
Birthplace (City, State, County, Country)					
Location of Birth Certificate					
Location of Adoption Documents					
Social Security Number					
Location of Social Security Card					
Driver's License Number and State					
Military Service: Country and Branch					
Military Rank					
Military Induction Date					
Military Discharge Date					
Military Citations					
Location of Military Documents					
Date of First Marriage					
First Spouse's Name					
Location of Marriage Certificate					
Date of Divorce, Annulment, Legal Separation, or Death					
Location of Documents					
Date of Second Marriage					
Second Spouse's Name					
Location of Marriage Certificate					
Date of Divorce, Annulment, Legal Separation, or Death					
Location of Documents					
Date of Third Marriage					
Third Spouse's Name					
Location of Marriage Certificate					

Date of Divorce, Annulment, Legal Separation, or Death					
Location of Documents					
Date of Death					
Location of Death Certificate					
Address					
Telephone(s)					
Email					
Other					
Other					
Other					

Additional Notes

4

Children

This section lists all young children—whether my own or others—for whom I regularly provide care. For my own children, the "Guardians and Property Managers" section just below lists the people who should be their primary caretakers following my incapacity or death.

Guardians and Property Managers

I have named the following people to serve as caretakers for my children. I have also noted the documents in which the caretaker has been named—for example, my will, living trust, another trust, or a life insurance policy.

Caretaker	Child's Name	Child's Name	Child's Name	Child's Name
Personal Guardian				
Alternate				
Document				
Property Manager				
Alternate				
Document				

Caretaker	Child's Name	Child's Name	Child's Name	Child's Name
Personal Guardian				
Alternate				
Document				
Property Manager				
Alternate				
Document				

Information About Children

The children listed below rely on me for care and support. Please help to fill in for me until new caregivers assume their roles.

4

Children

Child's Name and Contact Information	Date of Birth	Child's Relationship to Me	Type of Care

Additional Care Providers

Here, you'll find contact information for others who help with the children's care.

Child's Name	Care Provider or Family Member's Contact Information	Relationship to Child	Type of Care

4

Children

Child's Name	Care Provider or Family Member's Contact Information	Relationship to Child	Type of Care

Additional Care Providers, continued

Child's Name	Care Provider or Family Member's Contact Information	Relationship to Child	Type of Care

Additional Notes

5

Others Who Depend on Me

This section provides basic information about adults who depend on me for care.

Information About People Who Depend on Me

The people listed below rely on me for care and support. Please help to fill in for me until new caregivers assume their roles.

Person's Name and Contact Information	Date of Birth	Person's Relationship to Me	Type of Care

Additional Care Providers

The following people also provide care for the individuals listed above.

Person's Name	Care Provider's Contact Information	Relationship to Person	Type of Care

Person's Name	Care Provider's Contact Information	Relationship to Person	Type of Care

Additional Notes

6

Pets and Livestock

This section lists the animals I own and describes my wishes for their care and placement.

Animal Care

Pet Name, Chip ID, Species, and Coloring	Location	Food and Water	Other Care	Veterinarian's Contact Information

6

Pets and Livestock

Pet Name, Chip ID, Species, and Coloring	Location	Food and Water	Other Care	Veterinarian's Contact Information

Wishes for Placement

Pet Name, Chip ID, Species, and Coloring	Desired Placement	Individual or Organization and Contact Information

Pet Name, Chip ID, Species, and Coloring	Desired Placement	Individual or Organization and Contact Information

Additional Notes

7

Employment

In this section, you'll find information about my current and former employment, whether full time or part time, paid or volunteer. For every position I've listed, I've indicated whether or not benefits are available if I become incapacitated or die. (These benefits may be detailed elsewhere in this planner—for example, in the Insurance or Retirement Plans and Pensions sections—but I include them here so they will not be overlooked.)

Current Employment

Please contact my current employers if I become incapacitated or when I die. In addition to collecting any benefits due, if I have worked until the time of my incapacity or death, my agent or executor should ask my employer for any unpaid wages or commissions, expense reimbursements, or bonuses that are due to me or to my estate.

Employer's Contact Information	Current Benefits and Location of Documents	
	Position	
	Start Date	
	Ownership Interest	☐ Yes (_____%) ☐ No
Employer's Contact Information	Current Benefits and Location of Documents	
	Position	
	Start Date	
	Ownership Interest	☐ Yes (_____%) ☐ No
Employer's Contact Information	Current Benefits and Location of Documents	
	Position	
	Start Date	
	Ownership Interest	☐ Yes (_____%) ☐ No

7

Employment

Employer's Contact Information	Current Benefits and Location of Documents	
	Position	
	Start Date	
	Ownership Interest	☐ Yes (_____%) ☐ No
Employer's Contact Information	Current Benefits and Location of Documents	
	Position	
	Start Date	
	Ownership Interest	☐ Yes (_____%) ☐ No
Employer's Contact Information	Current Benefits and Location of Documents	
	Position	
	Start Date	
	Ownership Interest	☐ Yes (_____%) ☐ No

Additional Notes

Previous Employment

Employer's Contact Information	Current Benefits and Location of Documents	
	Last Position	
	Start and End Dates	
	Ownership Interest	☐ Yes (_____%) ☐ No
Employer's Contact Information	Current Benefits and Location of Documents	
	Last Position	
	Start and End Dates	
	Ownership Interest	☐ Yes (_____%) ☐ No
Employer's Contact Information	Current Benefits and Location of Documents	
	Last Position	
	Start and End Dates	
	Ownership Interest	☐ Yes (_____%) ☐ No
Employer's Contact Information	Current Benefits and Location of Documents	
	Last Position	
	Start and End Dates	
	Ownership Interest	☐ Yes (_____%) ☐ No
Employer's Contact Information	Current Benefits and Location of Documents	
	Last Position	

	Start and End Dates	
	Ownership Interest	☐ Yes (_____%) ☐ No
Employer's Contact Information	Current Benefits and Location of Documents	
	Last Position	
	Start and End Dates	
	Ownership Interest	☐ Yes (_____%) ☐ No
Employer's Contact Information	Current Benefits and Location of Documents	
	Last Position	
	Start and End Dates	
	Ownership Interest	☐ Yes (_____%) ☐ No

Additional Notes

_____

_____

_____

_____

_____

_____

_____

_____

_____

_____

_____

_____

_____

7

Employment

8

Business Interests

Following is an overview of my current and former business interests. It contains information to help you notify the right people (co-owners, employees, and so on) of my incapacity or death. Over time, this information will also help you manage or sell my business interests.

Current Business Interests

This section provides detailed information about businesses in which I have a current ownership interest.

Name and Location

Business Name and Type of Business	Main Office Address and Telephone	Subsidiaries or Branch Offices

Ownership

Business Owners	Contact Information	Job Title or Position	Ownership Percentage

Business Owners	Contact Information	Job Title or Position	Ownership Percentage

8

Business Interests

Ownership Documents	Location of Documents

Disposition

These instructions will help you manage or wind up my business affairs if I become incapacitated, or upon my death.

Disposition of Entire Business	☐ Continue	☐ Transfer	☐ Sell	☐ Liquidate
Disposition of My Interest		☐ Transfer	☐ Sell	☐ Liquidate

Contact Information for Key Individuals				
Attorney	Accountant			

Disposition Notes

Title and Location of Documents

8

Business Interests

Key Employees

This section lists employees who are essential to keeping the business running, or who have special agreements with the business.

Employee Name	Agreement	Location of Documents	Other Information

Business Taxes

Business tax records are located as follows:

Current-Year Records	
Prior-Year Records	

Significant Assets and Liabilities

This section lists important assets and liabilities, to help you manage, transfer, or sell the business.

Assets

Description of Asset	Location of Asset	Access Information	Contact Name and Information	Location of Documents

Description of Asset	Location of Asset	Access Information	Contact Name and Information	Location of Documents

8

Business Interests

Liabilities

Description of Liability	Contact Name and Information	Location of Documents

Description of Liability	Contact Name and Information	Location of Documents

Additional Notes

8

Business Interests

Prior Business Interests

My prior business interests are outlined below. My investments, rights, and responsibilities in these businesses have been fully resolved and terminated; no additional expenses will be incurred and no income realized. I have described these business interests for your reference, in case you have questions or receive any future claims.

Business Name and Type of Business	Main Office Address and Telephone	Ownership and Dissolution Documents	Location of Documents
Contact Information			

Business Name and Type of Business	Main Office Address and Telephone	Ownership and Dissolution Documents	Location of Documents
Contact Information			

Business Name and Type of Business	Main Office Address and Telephone	Ownership and Dissolution Documents	Location of Documents
Contact Information			

Additional Notes

8

Business Interests

9

Memberships and Communities

Following is a list of clubs, groups, programs, and organizations to which I belong. You may need this information to notify others of my incapacity or death, complete my obituary, cancel memberships, or transfer membership benefits.

Organization Name and Contact Information	Account Name, Password, Membership Number, or Position Held	Additional Notes

Organization Name and Contact Information	Account Name, Password, Membership Number, or Position Held	Additional Notes

Service Providers

My current service providers are listed below. This information may help you manage bills and expenses or provide ongoing care for me, my home, or my other property. Over time, you should cancel or modify these service arrangements, as necessary.

Health Care Providers

Name and Contact Information	Type of Care and Details

Name and Contact Information	Type of Care and Details

Name and Contact Information	Type of Care and Details

Other Service Providers

Name and Contact Information	Type of Service and Details

Name and Contact Information	Type of Service and Details

Name and Contact Information	Type of Service and Details

10

Service Providers

Additional Notes

Health Care Directives

In this section, you'll find information about documents I have made to direct my health care if I am incapacitated and unable to speak for myself.

Health Care Agent

In my health care documents, I have named the person listed below to be my health care agent. My agent will supervise my care if I am incapacitated. If he or she is unable to serve, I have named alternates to serve in the order listed.

Health Care Agent	
Alternate 1	
Alternate 2	
Alternate 3	

Health Care Documents

Following is basic information about my health care documents.

If an attorney or other professional helped me prepare a document listed here, I have included contact information for him or her. You can consult the listed professional if you have questions about the document or need help carrying out its terms.

Document Title	
Date Prepared	
Effective Date	☐ Immediately ☐ Upon my incapacity ☐ Other:
Professional Help	An attorney or other professional helped me prepare this document: ☐ Yes ☐ No
Professional's Name, Title, and Contact Information	
Location of Original Document	
Locations of Copies of This Document	
Additional Notes	

Document Title	
Date Prepared	
Effective Date	☐ Immediately　　☐ Upon my incapacity　　☐ Other:
Professional Help	An attorney or other professional helped me prepare this document: ☐ Yes　☐ No
Professional's Name, Title, and Contact Information	
Location of Original Document	
Locations of Copies of This Document	
Additional Notes	

Document Title	
Date Prepared	
Effective Date	☐ Immediately　　☐ Upon my incapacity　　☐ Other:
Professional Help	An attorney or other professional helped me prepare this document: ☐ Yes　☐ No
Professional's Name, Title, and Contact Information	
Location of Original Document	
Locations of Copies of This Document	
Additional Notes	

Durable Power of Attorney for Finances

This section contains information about my durable power of attorney for finances.

I have also listed any nondurable powers of attorney for finances I have made. Nondurable powers of attorney are no longer valid if I become incapacitated. Please destroy them.

If an attorney or other professional helped me prepare a document listed here, I have included contact information for him or her. You can consult the listed professional if you have questions about the document or need help carrying out its terms.

Durable Power of Attorney for Finances

The following document is durable, which means it remains effective after I am incapacitated and unable to manage my own affairs. All powers granted under the document terminate upon my death. For information about who has authority to handle my affairs after death, see Section 17, Will and Trust.

Document Title	
Date Prepared	
Agent's Name	
Alternate Agents' Names	
Effective Date	☐ Immediately ☐ Upon my incapacity ☐ Other:
Professional Help	An attorney or other professional helped me prepare this document: ☐ Yes ☐ No
Professional's Name, Title, and Contact Information	
Location of Original Document	
Locations of Copies of This Document	
Additional Notes	

Other Financial Power of Attorney

The following documents are not durable, which means that they are no longer valid if I become incapacitated. If possible, please locate and destroy all copies of these documents to prevent anyone from mistakenly taking action under them.

Document Title	
Date Prepared	
Agent's Name	
Alternate Agents' Names	
Effective Date	☐ Immediately ☐ Other:
Termination Date	☐ Upon my incapacity or death ☐ Other:
Professional Help	An attorney or other professional helped me prepare this document: ☐ Yes ☐ No
Professional's Name, Title, and Contact Information	
Location of Original Document	
Locations of Copies of This Document	
Additional Notes	

Document Title	
Date Prepared	
Agent's Name	
Alternate Agents' Names	
Effective Date	☐ Immediately ☐ Other:
Termination Date	☐ Upon my incapacity or death ☐ Other:
Professional Help	An attorney or other professional helped me prepare this document: ☐ Yes ☐ No
Professional's Name, Title, and Contact Information	
Location of Original Document	
Locations of Copies of This Document	
Additional Notes	

13

Organ or Body Donation

In this section, I have outlined my wishes and any arrangements I have made for donation of my remains. If I have chosen to donate my body, organs, or tissues, I have also selected either burial or cremation (outlined in the next section) to follow the donation or to be carried out in the event that the donation is not accepted. Please review this section along with Sections 14, 15, and 16 prior to making my final arrangements.

After my death, I want to donate my body, organs, or tissues: ☐ Yes   ☐ No

If "No," skip the rest of this section and turn to the next section.

Wishes for Donation

I would like to donate:	☐ My body
	☐ Any needed organs or tissues
	☐ Only the following organs or tissues:

Arrangements for Donation

Receiving Organization's Name, Address, and Telephone Number			
Location of Documents			
Additional Notes			

14

Burial or Cremation

In this section, I have outlined my wishes and any arrangements I have made for burial or cremation of my remains. Please review this section along with Sections 13, 15, and 16 prior to making my final arrangements.

Disposition of Remains

I have selected either burial or cremation, and have provided details about my wishes.

☐ **Burial**			
	Check One: ☐ Immediate ☐ After services	Check One: ☐ Embalm ☐ Do not embalm	Check One: ☐ In-ground ☐ Aboveground
Burial Organization Contact Information			
Burial Location and Contact Information			
Location of Documents			
Additional Notes			

☐ Cremation

Check One:	Check One:	Check One or All That Apply:	
☐ Immediate ☐ After services	☐ Embalm ☐ Do not embalm	☐ Niche in columbarium ☐ In-ground	☐ Scattered ☐ To individual

Cremation Organization Contact Information	
Final Location and Contact Information	
Location of Documents	
Additional Notes	

Casket or Urn

I would like a casket, urn, or other container to hold my remains: ☐ Yes ☐ No

Item	☐ Casket	☐ Urn	☐ Other
Material	☐ Wood Type: _____	☐ Metal Type: _____	☐ Other Type: _____
Model or Design			
Exterior Finish			
Interior Finish			
Cost Range	☐ Economical Approx. $_____	☐ Moderate Approx. $_____	☐ Luxury Approx. $_____
Additional Notes			

Item	☐ Casket	☐ Urn	☐ Other
Material	☐ Wood	☐ Metal	☐ Other
	Type: _____	Type: _____	Type: _____
Model or Design			
Exterior Finish			
Interior Finish			
Cost Range	☐ Economical	☐ Moderate	☐ Luxury
	Approx. $_____	Approx. $_____	Approx. $_____
Additional Notes			

Item	☐ Casket	☐ Urn	☐ Other
Material	☐ Wood	☐ Metal	☐ Other
	Type: _____	Type: _____	Type: _____
Model or Design			
Exterior Finish			
Interior Finish			
Cost Range	☐ Economical	☐ Moderate	☐ Luxury
	Approx. $_____	Approx. $_____	Approx. $_____
Additional Notes			

14

Burial or Cremation

Headstone, Monument, or Burial Marker

I would like a headstone or marker: ☐ Yes ☐ No

Description	
Material	
Design	
Finish	
Additional Notes	

Epitaph

I would like an epitaph or inscription: ☐ Yes ☐ No

Item	
Inscription	
Additional Notes	

Item	
Inscription	
Additional Notes	

Item	
Inscription	
Additional Notes	

14

Burial or Cremation

Burial or Cremation Apparel

I wish to specify burial or cremation apparel: ☐ Yes ☐ No

For items marked "Yes," please ensure that the clothing or article is removed and given to my executor prior to burial or cremation.

Clothing, Accessory, or Other Item	Location	Remove Before Interment or Cremation
		☐ Yes ☐ No
		☐ Yes ☐ No
		☐ Yes ☐ No
		☐ Yes ☐ No
		☐ Yes ☐ No
		☐ Yes ☐ No
		☐ Yes ☐ No
		☐ Yes ☐ No
		☐ Yes ☐ No
		☐ Yes ☐ No
		☐ Yes ☐ No
Additional Notes		

14

Burial or Cremation

Funeral and Memorial Services

In this section, I have outlined my wishes and any arrangements I have made for services or ceremonies after my death. Please review this section along with Sections 13, 14, and 16 prior to making my final arrangements.

Viewing, Visitation, or Wake

I would like a viewing, visitation, or wake: ☐ Yes ☐ No

Type of Service	
Location and Contact Information	
Existing Arrangements and Location of Documents	

Body Present	Casket	Casket
☐ Yes ☐ No	☐ Yes ☐ No	☐ Open ☐ Closed

Invitees ☐ Public ☐ Private	Timing and Days/Hours
Special Requests	
Additional Notes	

15

Funeral and Memorial Services

Type of Service	
Location and Contact Information	
Existing Arrangements and Location of Documents	

Body Present	**Casket**	**Casket**
☐ Yes ☐ No	☐ Yes ☐ No	☐ Open ☐ Closed

Invitees ☐ Public ☐ Private	**Timing and Days/Hours**

Special Requests	
Additional Notes	

Funeral or Memorial Service

I would like a funeral or memorial: ☐ Yes ☐ No

Location and Contact Information	
Existing Arrangements and Location of Documents	

Body and Casket Present	Casket	Other Items
☐ Yes ☐ No	☐ Open ☐ Closed	☐ Photo—Location: ☐ Other: _____
Flowers	**Invitees** ☐ Public ☐ Private	**Timing and Days/Hours**

Type of Service	Service Contact	Facilitator
☐ Religious	Name	Name
☐ Military		
☐ Other	Contact Information	Contact Information

Eulogy

Name	Name	Name
Contact Information	**Contact Information**	**Contact Information**

Music Selections and Musicians

Readings

Pallbearers

Name #1	Name #2	Name #3
Contact Information	**Contact Information**	**Contact Information**

Name #4	Name #5	Name #6
Contact Information	**Contact Information**	**Contact Information**

Pallbearers, continued

Name #7	Name #8	Name-Alternate
Contact Information	**Contact Information**	**Contact Information**
Name-Alternate	**Name-Alternate**	**Name-Alternate**
Contact Information	**Contact Information**	**Contact Information**

Graveside Ceremony	Transportation to Service
☐ Graveside only	
☐ Following funeral	
☐ None	

Additional Notes	

Reception or Celebration of Life

I would like a reception or celebration of life: ☐ Yes ☐ No

Location and Contact Information	
Existing Arrangements and Location of Documents	

Invitees	Food and Drink	
☐ Public ☐ Private		

Additional Notes	

Obituary

Please publish my obituary. ☐ Yes ☐ No

I have already drafted an obituary: ☐ Yes (Location: _____) ☐ No

If I have not drafted an obituary, please prepare one using the information and instructions below.

Obituary Overview

Obituary Length	☐ Brief	☐ Moderate	☐ Article Length
Photographs	☐ Yes (Location: _____)	☐ No	
Publications			

Obituary Details

Date and Place of Birth	See Biographical Information, Section 3
Military Service	See Biographical Information, Section 3
Spouse, Children, Grand-children, Parents, Siblings	See Biographical Information, Section 3
Employment and Business Interests	See Employment, Section 7, and Business Interests, Section 8
Memberships and Communities	See Memberships and Communities, Section 9
Education	
Awards and Achievements	
Interests and Hobbies	
Values	
Public or Private	See Funeral and Memorial Services, Section 15, for my wishes for *public* or *private* ceremonies—(1) viewing, visitation, or wake; (2) funeral or memorial service; and (3) reception or celebration of life.
Flowers	☐ Yes. Send to:
	☐ No. "No flowers, please."
	☐ No. "In lieu of flowers, please send donations to [the organizations listed below]."

Donations or Remembrances (Organization and Contact Information)	
Other	

Additional Notes

17

Will and Trust

In this section, you will find important information about my will. If I have made other estate planning documents, such as a living trust, other trusts, or a marital property agreement, you will find those listed here as well.

If an attorney or other professional (such as a tax expert) helped me prepare a document listed here, I have included contact information for him or her. You can consult the listed professional if you have questions about the document or need help carrying out its terms.

Document Title	
Date Prepared	
Professional Help	An attorney or other professional helped me prepare this document: ☐ Yes ☐ No
Professional's Name, Title, and Contact Information	
Location of Original Document	
Locations of Copies of This Document	
Executor or Successor Trustee	
Alternate 1	
Alternate 2	
Alternate 3	
Additional Notes	

Document Title	
Date Prepared	
Professional Help	An attorney or other professional helped me prepare this document: ☐ Yes ☐ No
Professional's Name, Title, and Contact Information	
Location of Original Document	
Locations of Copies of This Document	
Executor or Successor Trustee	
Alternate 1	
Alternate 2	
Alternate 3	
Additional Notes	

Document Title	
Date Prepared	
Professional Help	An attorney or other professional helped me prepare this document: ☐ Yes ☐ No
Professional's Name, Title, and Contact Information	
Location of Original Document	
Locations of Copies of This Document	
Executor or Successor Trustee	
Alternate 1	
Alternate 2	
Alternate 3	
Additional Notes	

Document Title	
Date Prepared	
Professional Help	An attorney or other professional helped me prepare this document: ☐ Yes ☐ No
Professional's Name, Title, and Contact Information	
Location of Original Document	
Locations of Copies of This Document	
Executor or Successor Trustee	
Alternate 1	
Alternate 2	
Alternate 3	
Additional Notes	

Document Title	
Date Prepared	
Professional Help	An attorney or other professional helped me prepare this document: ☐ Yes ☐ No
Professional's Name, Title, and Contact Information	
Location of Original Document	
Locations of Copies of This Document	
Executor or Successor Trustee	
Alternate 1	
Alternate 2	
Alternate 3	
Additional Notes	

17

Will and Trust

17

Will and Trust

Document Title	
Date Prepared	
Professional Help	An attorney or other professional helped me prepare this document: ☐ Yes ☐ No
Professional's Name, Title, and Contact Information	
Location of Original Document	
Locations of Copies of This Document	
Executor or Successor Trustee	
Alternate 1	
Alternate 2	
Alternate 3	
Additional Notes	

Document Title	
Date Prepared	
Professional Help	An attorney or other professional helped me prepare this document: ☐ Yes ☐ No
Professional's Name, Title, and Contact Information	
Location of Original Document	
Locations of Copies of This Document	
Executor or Successor Trustee	
Alternate 1	
Alternate 2	
Alternate 3	
Additional Notes	

18

Insurance

This section lists all my insurance policies. It covers policies that I own and those owned by others that cover my life or my property.

My agent or executor should review each listed policy and contact the insurance company to:

- claim any benefits due—for example, medical, workers' compensation, life, or accidental death
- cancel policies that are no longer necessary—such as medical, dental, or vision insurance, after my death, and
- modify policies—for instance, modifying my home or vehicle insurance policies after my death but before transferring the property to beneficiaries.

Type of Policy and Policy Number	Insurance Company Name and Contact Information	Policy Owner	Description of Coverage and Status	Location of Policy
Medical				
No.				
Medical				
No.				
Medical				
No.				

18

Insurance

Type of Policy and Policy Number	Insurance Company Name and Contact Information	Policy Owner	Description of Coverage and Status	Location of Policy
Medical				
No.				
Dental				
No.				
Dental				
No.				
Vision				
No.				
Vision				
No.				

Type of Policy and Policy Number	Insurance Company Name and Contact Information	Policy Owner	Description of Coverage and Status	Location of Policy
Home and Contents, Renters'				
No.				
Home and Contents, Renters'				
No.				
Vehicle				
No.				
Vehicle				
No.				
Vehicle				
No.				

18

Insurance

18

Insurance

Type of Policy and Policy Number	Insurance Company Name and Contact Information	Policy Owner	Description of Coverage and Status	Location of Policy
Vehicle				
No.				
Vehicle				
No.				
Umbrella Liability				
No.				
Personal Liability				
No.				
Personal Liability				
No.				

Type of Policy and Policy Number	Insurance Company Name and Contact Information	Policy Owner	Description of Coverage and Status	Location of Policy
Malpractice				
No.				
Malpractice				
No.				
Errors and Omissions				
No.				
Errors and Omissions				
No.				
Disability				
No.				

18

Type of Policy and Policy Number	Insurance Company Name and Contact Information	Policy Owner	Description of Coverage and Status	Location of Policy
Disability				
No.				
Disability				
No.				
Disability				
No.				
Life				
No.				
Life				
No.				

Type of Policy and Policy Number	Insurance Company Name and Contact Information	Policy Owner	Description of Coverage and Status	Location of Policy
Life **No.**				
Life **No.**				
Accidental Death **No.**				
Accidental Death **No.**				
Long-Term Care **No.**				

18

Insurance

Type of Policy and Policy Number	Insurance Company Name and Contact Information	Policy Owner	Description of Coverage and Status	Location of Policy
Long-Term Care				
No.				
Other				
No.				
Other				
No.				
Other				
No.				
Other				
No.				

18

Insurance

Type of Policy and Policy Number	Insurance Company Name and Contact Information	Policy Owner	Description of Coverage and Status	Location of Policy
Other				
No.				
Other				
No.				
Other				
No.				
Other				
No.				

Additional Notes

Bank and Brokerage Accounts

Following is a complete list of my bank and brokerage accounts. See my estate planning documents—that is, my durable power of attorney for finances, will, and/or living trust—for complete information about managing or distributing the funds in these accounts. Contact each financial institution to arrange account access according to the powers granted in my estate planning documents.

If I have named a pay- or transfer-on-death beneficiary for an account, I have included the beneficiary's name with the account information, below. Upon my death, the beneficiary can go to the financial institution with a certified copy of the death certificate and collect the assets, without probate proceedings.

At the end of the section, you will also find important contact information in case checks are lost or stolen.

Financial Institution Contact Information	Account Number, Description of Assets, and Pay- or Transfer-on-Death Beneficiary	Debit Card and Online Access	Location of Checkbook, Check Stock, and Statements

19

Bank and Brokerage Accounts

Financial Institution Contact Information	Account Number, Description of Assets, and Pay- or Transfer-on-Death Beneficiary	Debit Card and Online Access	Location of Checkbook, Check Stock, and Statements

Financial Institution Contact Information	Account Number, Description of Assets, and Pay- or Transfer-on-Death Beneficiary	Debit Card and Online Access	Location of Checkbook, Check Stock, and Statements

Additional Notes

_____

_____

_____

_____

_____

_____

_____

19

Bank and Brokerage Accounts

If Checks Are Lost or Stolen

If checks are lost, stolen, or misused, you should immediately contact the bank or brokerage for the account. Then file a police report.

If checks are unexpectedly denied by a merchant, ask the merchant for contact information for the check verification service being used. Follow up with the service to learn why the check was denied and resolve any errors or fraud.

To help you quickly resolve problems, here is consumer contact information for commonly used check verification services:

Chex Systems, Inc.
800-428-9623—for consumer assistance
www.chexsystems.com

CrossCheck, Inc.
800-843-0760—for consumer assistance
www.cross-check.com

First Data TeleCheck
800-366-2425—for declined checks
800-710-9898—for stolen checks or fraud
www.firstdata.com/telecheck

Retirement Plans and Pensions

This section describes my retirement plans and pension benefits. Notify the managing company or organization of my incapacity or death. Then evaluate each plan for amounts due to my estate or survivors.

When you are ready to distribute the funds to my beneficiaries, please share with them the following information. It is important that my beneficiaries understand how to handle an inherited retirement plan. If a plan isn't handled correctly, the law may require its funds to be withdrawn sooner, with income tax paid earlier, and this would significantly reduce the plan's value to each beneficiary. It would be wise for all of my beneficiaries—which could include my spouse, other family or friends, organizations, or (rarely) a trust—to get good advice about how to deal with inheriting these types of plans.

- **Spouse.** A beneficiary spouse is entitled to rights and tax breaks that other beneficiaries are not. For example, a spouse can roll the inherited amount into a traditional IRA or qualified employer plan, can postpone distributions to age 70½, or can choose to be treated as the plan beneficiary (not owner) for tax treatment of withdrawals.

- **Nonspouse individuals.** Each nonspouse beneficiary should set up a separate account that is titled with my name, date of death, and the beneficiary's name. As an example:

  Mary Melone (deceased May 31, 2016) IRA for the benefit of Eliza Heron

The beneficiary should request a trustee-to-trustee transfer directly to the new account.

Note that a beneficiary younger than I was can extend the minimum distribution schedule according to their life expectancy, providing that he or she starts taking "required minimum distributions" in the year following my death.

Employer Retirement and Pension Plans

Company Contact Information	Description, Status of Plan, and Beneficiary	Account Number and Online Access	Location of Statements

Company Contact Information	Description, Status of Plan, and Beneficiary	Account Number and Online Access	Location of Statements

Additional Notes

Individual Retirement Accounts and Plans

Financial Institution Contact Information	Description, Status of Plan, and Beneficiary	Account Number and Online Access	Location of Statements

Financial Institution Contact Information	Description, Status of Plan, and Beneficiary	Account Number and Online Access	Location of Statements

Additional Notes

Government Benefits

In this section, you'll find information about any federal or state government benefits that I either currently collect or expect in the future. These include any benefits for my family members and survivors.

Social Security Benefits

I have outlined my Social Security benefits below. Upon my incapacity or death, notify the Social Security Administration at 800-772-1213 or contact your local SSA office. You can locate the local office by calling the SSA number or checking the government listings in the phone book.

Review the status of my benefits and ask the SSA representative whether additional benefits are available to me or to my family. A one-time death benefit is normally available for qualifying survivors.

Information, publications, and forms are available at the Social Security Administration website, www.ssa.gov.

Program Name	Account Name and SSN	Account Access, Status, and Payment	Location of Documents
Retirement			
Disability			
Supplemental Security Income (SSI)			

Program Name	Account Name and SSN	Account Access, Status, and Payment	Location of Documents
Family			
Survivor			

Other Government Benefits

Following is a list of any other government benefits that I currently receive or expect in the future. For each program, notify the program administrator of my incapacity or death, review the status of my benefits, and discuss whether additional benefits are available to my family or to me.

Program Name and Contact Information	Program Description	Account Name and Identification	Account Access, Status, and Payment	Location of Documents

Program Name and Contact Information	Program Description	Account Name and Identification	Account Access, Status, and Payment	Location of Documents

Additional Notes

_____

_____

_____

_____

_____

_____

21

Credit Cards and Debts

This section contains information about my bills, credit cards, and other debts. At the end of the section, you will also find important contact information in case a credit card is lost or stolen.

Bill Storage and Payment

I store paper bills in the following location (until I pay them):

Location of Pending Bills	

The table below provides information about how I receive and pay each of my bills. For example, I might receive a bill through the mail or electronically, and I might pay a bill by check or money order, online, automatically by preauthorized charge to my credit card, or through an automatic debit to my bank account. This chart also tells you where I've stored records of paid bills.

For additional information about banking, see Section 19 of my planner. For more about online accounts and email, see Section 23.

Payee	Account Number	Notice	Frequency and Amount	Method of Payment	Record of Payment

Payee	Account Number	Notice	Frequency and Amount	Method of Payment	Record of Payment

Additional Notes

_____

_____

_____

_____

_____

_____

_____

_____

_____

_____

22

Credit Cards and Debts

Credit Cards

Following is a list of all my credit cards, including customer service contact information. Note that my debit or ATM cards are listed in Section 19, along with the associated accounts.

Issuer	Account Number and Access	Customer Service Telephone

Additional Notes

_____

_____

_____

_____

_____

_____

_____

Debts I Owe to Others

In addition to the bills and credit cards listed above, I owe the following debts:

Creditor Name and Contact Information	Amount	Terms of Debt and Status of Payment	Location of Documents

Additional Notes

Debts Others Owe to Me

Payment is due to me on the following debts:

Name and Contact Information	Amount	Terms of Debt and Status of Payment	Location of Documents

Name and Contact Information	Amount	Terms of Debt and Status of Payment	Location of Documents

Additional Notes

_____

_____

_____

_____

_____

If a Credit Card Is Lost or Stolen

If a credit card is lost or stolen, immediately contact the issuing company listed above. File a police report with the local police department. Then, to minimize the risk of identity theft and fraud, contact the organizations listed below.

Equifax Fraud Alert
866-349-5191
www.equifax.com
See link at bottom, "Request a fraud alert"

Experian Fraud Alert
888-397-3742
www.experian.com
See link at bottom, "Fraud Alert"

TransUnion Fraud Alert
800-680-7289
www.transunion.com
See tab, "Credit Report Assisstance,"
then "Fraud Alerts"

Social Security Fraud Hotline
Office of the Inspector General
800-269-0271
https://oig.ssa.gov/report

Federal Trade Commission
Complaint Assistant
877-438-4338
www.identitytheft.gov

Internal Revenue Service
Identity Protection
800-908-4490
www.irs.gov/identity-theft-fraud-scams/
identity-protection

Secured Places and Passwords

This section provides the information you will need to access property that I manage or store in secured places—including online accounts with passwords, physical items secured with combination locks, access codes, or keys, safe deposit boxes, and secret locations.

Products, Services, and Passwords

Product or Service	Account Name, User Name, or Account Number	Password, Combination, or PIN	Location of Key

Common Passwords

Here are some of my common passwords:			

Additional Notes

_____

_____

_____

_____

_____

_____

_____

Safe Deposit Boxes

If I am incapacitated. If I am incapacitated and you co-own a safe deposit box with me, your access rights are unaffected. If you do not already have access, however, you will need to meet special requirements before the financial institution will open a safe deposit box for you.

- If you are my agent for finances under a durable power of attorney, you will need to present the power of attorney document. If the document is a "springing" power of attorney, you will also need to present doctors' statements to verify that I am incapacitated.
- If you do not meet these requirements, you will need to obtain a court order to access a safe deposit box.

Upon my death. You will need to meet these special requirements before the financial institution will open a safe deposit box for you.

- If you are a co-owner on the box, your access will continue unimpeded unless the box is temporarily sealed (see below).
- If you are my executor or successor trustee, you will need to present a certified copy of my death certificate and a copy of the will or trust that names you to the job. (There may be a few weeks' delay, if the box is temporarily sealed. Again, see below.)
- If you meet none of these requirements, you will need to obtain a court order to access the safe deposit box.

Note that in some states, safe deposit boxes are sealed for a few weeks following the death of the owner so the state taxing authority can review the contents. During this time, you will not be able to obtain access to the box without a court order.

Here is a list of my safe deposit boxes:

Safe Deposit Boxes, continued

Bank Name and Contact Information	People With Authorized Access	Box Number and Location of Keys	Description of Contents

Secured Places and Passwords

Additional Notes

_____

_____

_____

_____

_____

_____

Other Keys

Additional keys are located as follows:

Purpose	Location

Other Assets, Other Locations

These items of personal property are on loan to others, hidden away, stored elsewhere, or known only to me—and I want you to be able to locate them after my death. I have also listed any personal property I have that is on loan to me from someone else. Please return these items to their owners.

Item and Description	Location of Asset	Location of Documents

Item and Description	Location of Asset	Location of Documents

Other Assets, Other Locations, continued

Item and Description	Location of Asset	Location of Documents

Secured Places and Passwords

Other Assets, Other Locations, continued

Item and Description	Location of Asset	Location of Documents

Additional Notes

Secured Places and Passwords

24

Taxes

The following information will help you prepare any tax returns due while I am incapacitated or after my death.

Tax Professionals

The following attorneys, accountants, or other professionals have helped me with my taxes in the past and are recommended to you for future work. Turn to them if you need assistance with my final tax returns.

Name of Person or Firm	Contact Information	Notes

Location of Tax Records

All receipts and documents related to income tax returns—both current-year records as well as prior-year returns—are located as described below.

Location of Current-Year Records	
Location of Prior-Year Records	

Additional Notes

Real Estate

Following is a list of all the real estate I own or rent, either solely or with others. This information will help you to manage the property in the short term and to sell or otherwise transfer the property when that becomes necessary.

If state law allows it, and I have named a transfer-on-death beneficiary for property I own, I have listed the beneficiary below. Please see the property deed for exact beneficiary designations, as I may have named multiple or alternate beneficiaries. Upon my death, the beneficiary should contact the land recorder's office in the county where the property is located. The beneficiary will need a certified copy of the death certificate to transfer the property; the recorder's office will tell the beneficiary exactly what steps to take.

Property I Own

Property Address	Mortgage Company Contact Information	Current Occupants and Contact Information	Transfer-on-Death Beneficiary	Location of Documents

Property Address	Mortgage Company Contact Information	Current Occupants and Contact Information	Transfer-on-Death Beneficiary	Location of Documents

25

Real Estate

Instructions for Care of Property I Own

Following are special instructions to help you care for the property listed above. If I hire someone to help with routine maintenance tasks, you can find that information in Section 10, Service Providers.

Property Address	Property Care

Property Address	Property Care

25

Real Estate

Additional Notes

Property I Rent or Lease

Property Address	Landlord's Contact Information	Term of Rental or Lease	Location of Documents

Instructions for Care of Leased or Rented Property

Following are special instructions to help you care for the property listed above. If I hire someone to help with routine maintenance tasks, you can find that information in Section 10, Service Providers.

Property Address	Property Care

Property Address	Property Care

Real Estate

25

Additional Notes

Vehicles

Here is a summary of all vehicles in which I hold an ownership or lease interest. This information will help you to manage the interest in the short term and to terminate, transfer, or sell the vehicle over time.

If state law allows it, and I have named a transfer-on-death beneficiary for a vehicle I own, I have included the beneficiary's name with the vehicle information, below. Upon my death, the beneficiary can go to the state motor vehicles department with a certified copy of the death certificate and transfer the vehicle title, without probate proceedings.

Vehicles I Own

Vehicle Type (Make, Model, Year, License Plate, and Vehicle ID Number)	Creditor Contact Information	Garage or Storage Location	Transfer-on-Death Beneficiary	Location of Documents

Vehicles

Vehicle Type (Make, Model, Year, License Plate, and Vehicle ID Number)	Creditor Contact Information	Garage or Storage Location	Transfer-on-Death Beneficiary	Location of Documents

26

Vehicles

Additional Notes

Vehicles I Lease

Vehicle Type (Make, Model, Year, License Plate, and Vehicle ID Number)	Leaseholder Contact Information	Garage or Storage Location	Location of Documents

Vehicles I Lease, continued

Vehicle Type (Make, Model, Year, License Plate, and Vehicle ID Number)	Leaseholder Contact Information	Garage or Storage Location	Location of Documents

Additional Notes

_____

_____

_____

_____

_____

_____

Other Income and Personal Property

This section describes sources of income and important items of personal property that aren't listed in other sections of my planner, and it tells you where to find warranty records and maintenance guides for items of personal property. It also details any property that I expect to receive in the future.

Other Income

Following is a list of income sources not described elsewhere in my planner:

Source and Contact Information	Description	Location of Documents

Other Income, continued

Source and Contact Information	Description	Location of Documents

Other Income & Personal Property

Other Income, continued

Source and Contact Information	Description	Location of Documents

Additional Notes

Other Personal Property

The following items of property are particularly valuable to me. For certain items, I have included instructions for special handling and/or noted whether I have named a beneficiary in my will or other estate planning document.

Item and Description	Location and Access Information	Special Instructions	Location of Documents

Item and Description	Location and Access Information	Special Instructions	Location of Documents

27

Other Income & Personal Property

Additional Notes

_____

_____

_____

_____

_____

_____

_____

_____

Property I Expect to Receive From Others

Following is a list of property that I expect to receive in the future. However, if I am named to receive property under a will, trust, or other estate planning document, and I die before I receive it, the property probably won't pass to my estate. Instead, it will most likely go to the benefactor's alternate beneficiary.

Source and Contact Information	Description	Location of Documents

Property I Expect to Receive From Others, continued

Source and Contact Information	Description	Location of Documents

Other Income & Personal Property

Property I Expect to Receive From Others, continued

Source and Contact Information	Description	Location of Documents

Additional Notes

_____

_____

_____

_____

_____

_____

_____

_____

_____

_____

_____

_____

_____

27

Other Income & Personal Property

Warranty Records and Product Guides

Warranty information, product guides, and repair records for my personal property are located as follows:

Other Information

This section includes any information and materials that didn't fit neatly into other sections of my planner.

Index

B

C

M

Mail, instruction section addressing, 22

Make-A-Wish Foundation, donating frequent flyer miles to, 74

Marital property agreements, 148, 154, 221

Marriage certificates

  in biographical information section, 33, 38

  informational vs. certified copies, 33

  locating, help with, 33

Married couples

  biographical information, 38

  estate taxes, 142

  financial agent, selection of, 98

  health care directives and, 83

  legal separation certificate, 33–34, 38

  marital property agreements, 148, 154, 221

  property ownership and, 220–222, 223

  separate planners for, 11

  See also Divorce; Marriage certificates

Match account, disposition of, 72

Medicaid, 165, 169

Medical directive. *See* Health care directives

Medical Orders for Scope of Treatment (MOST), 87

Medicare

  FICA (Social Security and Medicare) taxes, 188

  health care benefits, 188

  long-term care and, 165, 169

Memberships and communities, 70–75

  binder, materials to file in, 75

  charitable, 71

  civic, 70

  consumer, 71

  educational, 70–71

  fraternal and service groups, 71

  frequent flyer miles, transfers of, 73–74

  instruction section addressing, 23

  online accounts, disposition of, 71–73

  planner pages, 75

  professional, 70

  recreational, 71

  religious, spiritual or healing, 71

  resources to assist, 74–75

  reviewing and updating, 75

  social, 71

  survivors, transfer of benefits to, 73

Memorial services

  binder, materials to file in, 134

  cremation and, 112

  funeral services, distinguished, 127

  instruction section addressing, 21–22

  location of, 129

  planner pages, 131–133

  receptions or celebrations of life, 129, 133–134

  resources to assist, 129–130

  reviewing and updating information, 134

  types of, 129

  See also Funeral services; Viewing, visitation or wake

Mental health care directives, 87

Microsoft account, disposition of, 72

Military personnel

  deployment, and necessity of creating planner, 5

  funerals, 127, 132, 133

  Presidential Memorial Certificate, 114, 133

  veterans, burial and cremation benefits for, 114, 129

  See also Military records

Military records

  in biographical information section, 34–36, 38

  historical records, 35–36

  locating, help with, 34–36

  older records, 35

  recent records, 34–35

sturdy three-inch binder

three high-capacity angled D-rings

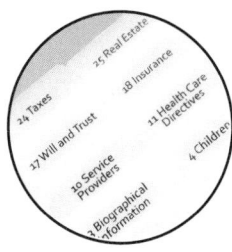

28 white Mylar-reinforced tab dividers

The *Get It Together* Binder & Tab Set

A Companion to *Get It Together*

The *Get It Together* **Binder & Tab Set** is a great place to store the personal planner you will create, along with all of your related materials—birth certificate, title to your car, real estate deeds, passwords, insurance policies, health care directive, will, trust, and more. With a binder, it's easy for you to organize and get to your records. And, when the time comes, the binder will be a handy reference for your family.

The binder is sky-blue matte vinyl, with dimensions of 11.75" x 11.75" x 3.13"; the tabs are 8.5" x 11" with 0.5" tab extensions.

For more information and to purchase, please visit Amazon.com and search for "get it together binder and tab set."

 **NOLO** *Online Legal Forms*

Nolo offers a large library of legal solutions and forms, created by Nolo's in-house legal staff. These reliable documents can be prepared in minutes.

Create a Document

- **Incorporation.** Incorporate your business in any state.
- **LLC Formations.** Gain asset protection and pass-through tax status in any state.
- **Wills.** Nolo has helped people make over 2 million wills. Is it time to make or revise yours?
- **Living Trust (avoid probate).** Plan now to save your family the cost, delays, and hassle of probate.
- **Trademark.** Protect the name of your business or product.
- **Provisional Patent.** Preserve your rights under patent law and claim "patent pending" status.

Download a Legal Form

Nolo.com has hundreds of top quality legal forms available for download—bills of sale, promissory notes, nondisclosure agreements, LLC operating agreements, corporate minutes, commercial lease and sublease, motor vehicle bill of sale, consignment agreements and many, many more.

Review Your Documents

Many lawyers in Nolo's consumer-friendly lawyer directory will review Nolo documents for a very reasonable fee. Check their detailed profiles at **Nolo.com/lawyers**.

 **NOLO** *Save 15%* off your next order

Register your Nolo purchase, and we'll send you a
coupon for 15% off your next Nolo.com order!

Nolo.com/customer-support/productregistration

On Nolo.com you'll also find:

Books & Software

Nolo publishes hundreds of great books and software programs for consumers and
business owners. Order a copy, or download an ebook version instantly, at Nolo.com.

Online Legal Documents

You can quickly and easily make a will or living trust, form an LLC or corporation, apply
for a trademark or provisional patent, or make hundreds of other forms—online.

Free Legal Information

Thousands of articles answer common questions about everyday legal issues
including wills, bankruptcy, small business formation, divorce, patents, employment,
and much more.

Plain-English Legal Dictionary

Stumped by jargon? Look it up in America's most up-to-date source for definitions
of legal terms, free at nolo.com.

Lawyer Directory

Nolo's consumer-friendly lawyer directory provides in-depth profiles of lawyers all
over America. You'll find all the information you need to choose the right lawyer.

GET8